A Divine Appointment

A Divine Appointment

JANICE KNUTH GORDON

A Divine Appointment

Copyright © 2020 by Janice Knuth Gordon. All rights reserved.

No part of this publication may be reproduced, stored in a retrieval system or transmitted in any way by any means, electronic, mechanical, photocopy, recording or otherwise without the prior permission of the author except as provided by USA copyright law.

The opinions expressed by the author are not necessarily those of URLink Print and Media.

1603 Capitol Ave., Suite 310 Cheyenne, Wyoming USA 82001
1-888-980-6523 | admin@urlinkpublishing.com

URLink Print and Media is committed to excellence in the publishing industry.

Book design copyright © 2020 by URLink Print and Media. All rights reserved.

Published in the United States of America

ISBN 978-1-64753-095-2 (Paperback)
ISBN 978-1-64753-096-9 (Digital)

06.01.20

If you have ever felt alone, hopeless, or suicidal, there IS hope. If you have ever felt you don't matter in the scheme of life, you will find you do. If you have wondered if what you believe in your heart really makes a difference, you will see that it does.

Do you ever feel like your whole world is crumbling down in a million pieces? Do you ever feel like everything is being snatched from the ground beneath you? Life is full of surprises –some are good, but others are not so good. Author Janice Knuth-Gordon using her my own firsthand life experiences, to show you there IS hope for the future and promises that are waiting to be fulfilled for your life. An inheritance bought and paid for.

Thank you to Jean Burns who brought me
to the realization of God's Word.

Dedication

I dedicate this book to all who feel their life is without reason, hope, or future. May you awaken in truth and feel abundant and hopeful and look to tomorrow with laughter, love, and longing.

Introduction

Is God real? Does it matter who we believe in?

How do we know? I always wanted to have proof of the truth. The story began as far back as I can remember. This book tells how I was shown those answers.

Regression

There are a multitude of situations that interfere with our emotional well-being. I recall sleeping in a small bedroom; my door opened into an upstairs hallway. Only one window in the room overlooked the river. On a moonlit night, I could see the water ripples reflecting in silver and the train trestle shining in the glow. My room was centered between by brothers' and sister's rooms at the top of a long, dark staircase. I was often afraid to go to bed, especially in the dark. It made me feel isolated and alone.

I know there are monsters under the bed. As soon as I put my feet over the side, they will get me! If only my mother knew how I needed her. If only she could comfort my fear, I would think to myself.

I had a little nightlight, but it was oh so dark beyond my tiny room facing the river. I often heard the mournful wailing of the train that ran along the river behind the house we lived in. I felt so alone. I prayed the angel of God prayer every night that my mother taught me, "Angel of God my guardian dear to whom God's love commits me here, ever this day be at my side to light and guard, to rule and guide. Amen" When I was frightened I would repeat it over and over. I was sure if I tried to run down the stairs to my mom the monsters would get me before I reached the bottom. I did not know I could put my faith in a living God.

Many memories of fear and loneliness begin during youth. However, these memories tend to become patchy with time. We all personalize our memories. Even when several of us experience the same situation, there will be memories depicting many different versions, depending on the stage of maturity and manner of the person experiencing it. Right now, you are thinking of one. What does it evoke in you? Tears? Heartache? Anger? It is so common to remember sad or painful situations while forgetting happy ones.

We have a choice: to use those memories to grow stronger or let them keep us in bondage. Learning to do this takes an understanding. All things are possible when you allow yourself the opportunity to meet the Creator of each one of us. He is waiting and desires to have a personal relationship with you. It is okay to feel anger, hate, revenge, sadness, pity, but it is *not* okay to let these things interrupt your life and the happiness you may attain.

God can change hearts. God can heal when we can no longer even think of forgiveness. God can turn any situation into a learning experience and fill us with peace and the strength to take one more step. He will never leave you, even if you yell and scream at Him. He loves you so much that he will wait for you to come to Him in love. When you feel no one cares or that no one loves you, He will always be there. You were in His thoughts long before you were born. He knew your mistakes before you made them. He wanted you here. He has a plan for you when you are ready to accept his guidance. He will gently lead you through. He is faithful. Just try Him; you will be amazed. He is all we need. Without Him feelings and painful memories can ruin our lives.

Feelings seem to control our needs, especially during childhood. Children must feel loved, wanted, worthy. A child doesn't understand when there is loneliness or an ache in the heart for a long hug from Mom. Children feel worth from affirmation from parents and siblings. It is well documented that a positive, loving reinforcement is necessary for healthy growth and development. It seemed natural that my needs were often looked after by my older siblings. My sister, four years my senior, was "turn-to" playmate in my preschool years, but my oldest brother, ten years my senior, seemed to be more of a caregiver. He often dressed me for the out-doors and kept me entertained. One summer day, he took me for a ride in the river in his rowboat, I sat on an inverted coffee can and bailed water with another one. We stayed among the rushes. I was never afraid when

I was with him. Another time I recall is when my older sister was outside picking grass in the backyard for our brother's guinea pig. She was around seven years old. He was throwing rocks and didn't see her, and one rock hit her on the top of the head. She came running to the house with blood running down her face and over her long light-blue coat. Mom rushed to her and whisked her away. Big brother watched over me. I felt sad that my sister was hurt but also that my brother got into trouble; I was sure he didn't mean it. Although my second eldest brother did nice things for me, my early childhood seemed to remember more times with my eldest brother.

My older sister often played with me, taught me many things, and would make up silly stories, like saying she was adopted. Around age three or four, when I was afraid, I would sneak into her room in the middle of the night while in my flannel "jammies" with the apple prints on them and climb into her bed. I got in trouble for doing that. I didn't know Mom was trying to protect her. My sister would awaken in a wet bed, and Mom thought this was a stigma on the family. Mom had her hands full with a son and my sister having this problem. My older siblings fill my childhood memories the most. One would think that the parents would.

My parents had a busy life. I was fifth in a chain of eight children. I did not know my parents had lost a three-month-old baby girl two years before I was born. As for my daddy, it seemed he was gone most of the day. He left early and came home late. I always looked forward to playing with him. In the winter, I would sit on his ice skates with my feet out in front of me when he was skating. When he took me ice fishing, I was so bundled up that all I could do was sit on an inverted pail and watch the boys catch fish. At home Dad would let me ride on his back and sit with him. He made me feel very special. He was very demonstrative with his affections.

Mom was not very affectionate. I did not know she had grown up without parents, that she had been shuffled here and there among her relatives along with her sister and two brothers who were separated from her. She had never had the love she needed as a child. She loved to dance and sing, and she played the harmonica. She even allowed me to blow on it, and we would sing together. She cleaned and washed clothes daily with the wringer washer and hung them in the basement when she could not hang them out of doors. She baked bread and always let us children play with some of the dough. The scent of fresh bread is still a strong initiator of my childhood memories. Although she was usually busy, one year we watched the Fourth of July fireworks down by the river's edge from the tracks, sitting on a yellow putt-putt car. This stands out as the only time --a special time --Mom shared with just me. She had her arm around me as we watched the beautiful colors erupt into the night sky reflecting in the river. I grew up feeling she didn't have time for me; however, memory is *not* failsafe. We need to be careful with memories. As I mentioned, memories can be skewed and selective according to our emotional status at the time of the memory and also over time, depending on how we feed it.

One thing I know, faith and the Catholic religion were a main theme in our home. Mom always told me how God knew everything we said and thought and how we were to be punished for doing bad things. She taught us m any prayers and always prayed on her knees-sometimes silently but usually aloud so we children could join in. They were prayers that we had memorized, along with the rosary. I was afraid of God. I prayed to my guardian angel every morning and night, even leaving a place for her to sleep on my pillow. I was taught to pray to saints, because I thought this practice was because you weren't to bother God as we are so I insignificant. (I am so glad that now I know, even though we are insignificant, I can take my concerns to Him anytime. This is true. God loves me and sent His Son to die for my sin so that I may share in His glory in heaven *forever!*) I recall that when Mom was worried about bad things, she told me all about heaven and hell and how we get punished for any bad thoughts we have or deeds we do. This made me very afraid of God and what could happen to me. How often we allow the evil spirit of fear to control us. Stop and think of your own experience. I had a lot to learn. When I went to first grade in parochial school, the sisters reinforced my fear of God. During the childhood years, they were awesome figures dressed in swirling, long black habits, veils, and funny shoes. The huge starchy white bib and forehead cover rustled when they moved. A huge black,

shiny rosary dangled at their waistline. Mystery surrounded their activities within the convent. "God will get you for anything bad you do!" This statement seemed to ring in my ears constantly. Stern, these nuns did not seem to portray the mercy their Order imparted.

Indoctrination Of Rituals

Catholicism was a dominant factor in our family. Mass came before school every morning. It was said in Latin. I only knew that the fragrance of the incense, the language, and the music seemed to lull me into heaven, gazing at the life-sized figurines of Mary, Joseph, Jesus, and saints (who were only those people who suffered to serve the Lord). I was taught that only people like us, who practiced Catholicism, were good and heaven - bound. We were discouraged to even associate with non-Catholics. Anyone who broke the laws of the church was hell-bound for sure!

It seemed that illness and injury were seen as punitive measures by God Himself to purify the soul so it could get to heaven. Of course, you could never suffer enough or be pure enough to go to heaven- that is why purgatory exited, to burn the rest of the sin off the soul so one could then enter the heavenly realm in purity. The 'big' sins, call "mortal" or "sacrilege," well, they sent you right to hell. This is why I was so afraid of God. I tried to do things right all the time, but sometimes my child behavior I new was wrong. No matter what behavior, I knew I would never be good enough to go to heaven. Is there something in your life that promotes that feeling? Did you know that without Jesus, *none* of us could get to heaven? He is just as close as your next breath. His Holy Spirit is *in* that breath. Close your eyes and take a deep breath through your nose and blow it out slowly from your mouth, using a pursed kissing motion. See, life is in that breath! He gives it to you. Get to know Him, love

Him, accept His sacrifice for you, and you can get a life-one that lasts *forever*, no matter what you have done in the past.

We all went to confession each week to tell the priest our sins. This was a ritual that was always difficult to obey, even for a child. We would watch the grown-ups come out of the little booth, kneel and pray devoutly, and would wonder what they had told the priest.

No one taught me about the mercy Christ has for us. I only knew at times my behavior was something I was ashamed of. I still remember in fourth grade a girl dropped her lunch money. I helped pick up the coins from the floor for her, but withheld a dime. Fifty-three years later, I still feel ashamed of that act. Ten cents went a long way in the 1950's. Even though I have asked for forgiveness, I did not know mercy was available for my bad behavior.

Behavior tends to be more human than divine. Jesus covered all sin with blood—His precious blood. You are forgiven. All you need is to ask Him, live for Him. You can do nothing without Him. He has given you talents unique for you alone. He will not force you. He wants you to come to Him in love. It is so easy – yet we make things so hard. If something seems easy, we look for the hidden agenda. I used to do that when I took tests. *Can't be that obvious,* I would think. Yet it was.

We all sin—*all* of us. The Word of God tells us in Romans 3:23, "... All fall short..." with the exception of Jesus. You see, I believed what was taught me: Suffering was a way of "cleansing" so you could go to heaven. Pain and prayers were something you could "offer up" to purify your soul or someone else's. So being a child who was stricken with pneumonia several times during a year left me feeling first I was really bad, and second it was necessary for me to be ill.

What do you think about Jesus? When did you form those opinions? What were those opinions based on? Truth? Someone else's opinion? That is why you must go to the truth in God's Word, the Bible, for answers. Ask Him to help you and *find His love*. It is right there all around you, waiting to absorb into your heart. I did not understand this growing up. The Bible says there is *ONE* Mediator to the Father, and that is Jesus Christ Himself. But I was taught to pray through the saints.

Prayer was taught as a form of ritual. Through memorization and repetition, they became imbedded into our minds. We perform rituals in many aspects of our lives. These have an impact on the decisions we make in life, from brushing our teeth to how we eat our food, even to how we pray. These things form patterns as we mature and can influence what we think about ourselves. In the Catholic faith, during the fifties, we were taught to pray to an intercessor –that is, a person who has been canonized through the Roman Catholic Church as a saint. There are patron saints of many kinds and statues that depict them.

Novenas are repetitive prayers said in succession for many days to the patron saint of your choice in hopes that, when it has been completed, the prayer request will be fulfilled. This ritual made me feel as though I was not able to speak to God and ask Him for what I needed. This has an effect on a child, making him or her feel quite worthless. O course, God is so holy and supreme, Why would He be bothered with a child's prayer?

Choosing a saint to pray for what I wanted or needed was embedded in my mind. I was taught certain delivered the results. It seemed no one was listening. I did not know Jesus wanted to hear from me. I thought God was someone way out there in heaven too busy to listen to a child.

I was indoctrinated with a belief about prayer that was false. When we are children, we absorb what is around us, and it becomes part of our core belief system. It is difficult to overcome these beliefs when it is not the truth. I was taught only the priest could interpret the Bible. I did not know God gave His Word for me to read.

The Bible tells us, "Do not be anxious about anything, but in everything, by prayer and petition, with thanksgiving, present your requests to God" (Philippians 4:6). As a child I was fearful of many things. I would wake up in the middle of the night in a panic, and no one could understand what the cause was. I would cry out to the saints, but nothing helped. I felt so lost and alone. I would hold my little plastic statue of Jesus and just cry. After my oldest brother was killed, I was hospitalized for swollen glands in the throat, and no one came to see me. No person tried to comfort me that worked there. I

A DIVINE APPOINTMENT

cried from loneliness and fear. I wanted to know who this Jesus was. I wanted to know if I mattered to Him. Why wasn't He listening? I heard older folks talk about dying and heaven after my brother died, and I wanted to go there too. I felt so empty.

God opens eyes and hearts when the desire is there. By the time I was a young teen I was so confused I begged Him to show me the truth. I was amidst all kinds of ideas –new age, humanism, that 'god' is whoever you want him to be, that every culture had a 'god' that should be accepted. I was taught early on about hell. The fear gave me a desire to delve into several different beliefs, and I prayed that the Lord would give me discernment to know the truth. I did believe in the Trinity and that Jesus was born to redeem us on the cross. I wanted to know who He was. I wanted to be loved by Him. I struggled with guilt for not practicing the Catholic law. I felt so unworthy that one Sunday, I went to mass and stayed outside the church on my knees begging forgiveness for my sins. I just talked to God from my heart instead of repeating the prayers I had learned and wept. I think that is when I truly accepted Him as my Savior.

Think about; we call a loved one on the phone to let them know we care. For God we need to pick up the Bible for a line to communicate.

He knows are hearts. When you read and study the Bible with a hunger for knowledge and a closer relationship with Jesus, the Spirit will fill you with what you need and desire. Prayer is something from the heart to the Beloved One who wants to hear from you. Just talk to Him.

It took years to overcome the false teachings about prayer. Many people swore that their prayers were answered *because* they prayed to a patron saint. Now I know there is only one God yet three persons within that deity–separate but one, all knowing, all being, feeling everyone's pain, forgiving everyone's sin who asks and receives Him. No human being who has died has the ability to read our minds. No saint, not even the Blessed Virgin Mary, can be in all places and hear all our prayers. *Only God can.* The Bible teaches us only Jesus can go to the Father for us, and He does willingly. The Father sees His beloved Son and His sacrifice to save us instead of our wretched selves. The blood of Christ makes us clean; Jesus said that He stood in our place and opens the way to heaven when we receive Him as our Savior. He tells us to pray in faith that He shall bless us one way or another. He loves to hear our prayers; He loves to bless us. Trust Him. He said to pray as if you already have the answer. *He* makes it easier to accept the path we travel, knowing *He* is in charge and never leaves us. He has proven this time and time again through my years, even when I did not understand it. He was communicating to me.

Strange Insights

I would periodically experience uneasy feelings beginning in my childhood and throughout my adult life. I would wake up with a lot of anxiety and did not understand why I felt this doom. It took several years before I would link this with an impending death or severe crisis. As a child, I was not aware of what I needed or what I should do when this anxiety occurred. The first time was when our neighbor lady passed away —we called her grandma S. She lived next door and was in her nineties. Her daughter cared for her, and her granddaughter lived upstairs in the same house. This feeling happened without warning and was unsettling. Since then, I have realized this occurred before someone I love died or, a crisis happened, usually within a few days.

As I grew older, I knew why, depending on the intensity of the feeling. I could tell if it was going to happen to someone really close to me or just an acquaintance. Sometimes it was just that something was wrong. I didn't know how to react to this at first. I was able to discern this feeling and learned to pray protection over whomever it was that needed it —to ask God to send angels to protect and build a hedge around whoever it was that needed to be lifted up and saved.

These are some of the outstanding premonitions that occurred over the years. I went on a boat ride with my sister-in-law. While she was sunning on the deck, I put my hand on her arm and I felt the strong premonition of doom. A few days later, she went in for surgery. She was twenty-six years old and died a few days after surgery. That same year, I was unable to sleep due to that feeling, that premonition again. I told my husband, "Someone I love is going to die." The next day we received a phone call. A neighbor's son was found dead on the tractor in the middle of the field. He was checking his traps and they ascertained the shotgun was on his lap and fell and went off as it fell off the tractor fatally wounding him. This boy was twenty-one years old, close to my age, and he had lived with us for several months after returning home from Viet Nam. Another time the feeling returned, but not as strong—usually that meant someone I knew, but not too close to me. My estranged husband's nephew was in the army, and he was killed in an accident. This premonition happened again prior to my father's death. I wrote him a letter, but he died before he received it, just five days after the birth of my second son. This was the hardest thing I had experienced at the time. I cried out to God and wanted to know my dad was alive in heaven. I cried from the depths of my soul and said, "You promised! My dad believed! I want to believe it is true too."

We were taking my father-in-law up North. We stopped in a shop and I looked at some beautiful gifts. I was thinking of a close friend we played cards with. I picked up a box and something inside said, "No she won't need this" so I place it back on the shelf. That night I was awake with that awful feeling. In the morning my daughter called and said my friend died that morning. We immediately came home.

Again, when a dear younger friend of mine was in final stages of breast cancer, I was visiting my sister. I awoke at 3:30 a.m. and knew my friend was there with me. I could feel her presence, and she said good-bye. I told her I would see her later and that I loved her while I wept.

I thanked God for this encounter. This was a personal glorious feeling. The next day I went home and told my husband she was gone, and that evening her husband notified us she passed at 3:30 a.m. In all, I knew God would direct my prayer of protection and safety to whom it was needed at the time of the occurrence. I could never ascertain why I had these premonitions. I always was a person of deep emotions. I did learn to trust in God and know somehow, someway, my prayer for the person or situation might facilitate some good that God had ordained. I am blessed in so many ways and am learning the importance of recognizing this premonition and immediately go to prayer. I am so thankful in knowing how to pray to my beloved Lord, to ask for help and mercy for myself and others in need. Do you ever feel urges to help someone out of the blue? That is God.

Needs

It seems at a young age, I longed to feel loved (something each of us desire). I recall one time as a small child, I thought about running out in front of a car and getting hurt so my mom would give me more attention, just for me. (Like when my sister was hit in the head with the rock). I did not realize at age four how dangerous this was. One day, while riding in the backseat, I did manage to open the door before the car totally stopped in the driveway, and I fell out. Mom rushed to my side but scolded me for being a "little dummy". I thought it was because she didn't love me.

Children think so differently than adults. We must never lose the ability to understand that fact. We never had much, but we were fed, clothed, and kept very clean. I loved it when Mom would hold me and dry my hair after a bath, her arms holding me close to her. Mom did what she thought was best. I cannot remember being rocked or read to; if at happened I was too young to recall. It seems my oldest brother was the one to comfort me when I fell, protected me when I was outdoors, and read to me when I was tired. There was a strong bond between us. This also created an even stronger need for acceptance when my brother was no longer available to me as I grew older.

Being accepted is not only important for children, but to every human being. During grade school, we had small classes, and we had our favorite buddies. My best girl friend had a brother the same age as my younger brother. When the boys got in to a fist fight at age four, I stood in the middle and tried to break it up. My friend and I ended up fist fighting instead. Of course, all the other kids were rooting for her. It was a bit of a stalemate, and we ended up even closer friends. I always felt sorry for the underdog and often put myself in the middle to save others. My pride was hurt more that anything else because some of the people I thought were my friends did not root for me, but at least my brother didn't suffer any effects. I was happy to take his blows. Now I know there is someone else who takes mine.

Punitive Damages

Every winter brought fear; I would be very ill with upper respiratory problems. My mom would put me on the couch with a tent made of a sheet over me an pump a vaporizer into the tent to help me break up my bronchial pneumonia. I would have severe congestion. I would be covered with Vicks and a cloth around my neck and over my chest. I would cough until I thought I would never breathe again. I still hate the smell of Vicks!

My mom would keep a close eye on me during my illnesses. I never knew her fear of losing a child. I thought I was suffering because I had to pay for my sins, even at age three or four. This implanted guilt and the idea of punishment as the result to pay for my wrongdoings. This continued for many years.

Results seem to continue from the situations that occur throughout our lives. Reflecting, one made a major impact on me. When I turned age twelve, my oldest brother was home on leave from the service. He woke me up and carried me downstairs on his shoulders on my birthday, and I received a stuffed Scottie dog for my present. I associated this gift with my brother. I held it close to remind me of him. He was discharged from the Navy later and then the following Spring, he was involved in a car accident. I had that anxious feeling again. I was devastated. I had prayed for God to heal him. I promised to be good. Mom took me with her to see him in the hospital. He drifted in and out of consciousness. He made the sign of the cross under the oxygen tent, opened his eyes, and hugged me, then drifted off again. Mom and I didn't stay long. A few days later, I was awakened by the sound of men coming to the front door. My mother came up and woke my older sister, and I pretended to be asleep. I crept quietly down the stairs and hid behind the sofa. The men told my mom my brother had passed away and gave her a bag with his belongings in it. I watched my Mom pull out the soiled, bloody clothes from the bag as she broke down sobbing. My dad was asleep, and Mom and my sister just cried. I snuck back upstairs, and buried my head in my pillow and cried out to the Lord, "*Why didn't you save my brother?*" Didn't He hear my prayer? I felt that familiar feeling; insignificant, alone again. That night, I had a dream where my brother came to me and gave me a big hug and said he was alright –I still can feel that hug. It seemed so real, and it gave me peace.

Throughout this ordeal, no one acknowledged the grief of a little girl, and this affected me the rest of my life. I was no one. People would pass me by at the funeral home to console my older brother and sister, Mom and Dad. My feelings did not seem to matter. How I ached in my soul. How could God do this? I had begged to have my brother healed.

My mom and dad were never the same. A few months later, my remaining older brother left for the air force, and I wept bitterly. Seems like yesterday. It all feels so unreal at times, yet the resulting deep pain of this little child is still mine.

A Question Of Truth

Once we attain a certain age, we feel our decisions are based on maturity and experience, not some obscured pain. During my teen years, I would inquire of god the whole meaning of *who I was* and *why I was*. I wanted proof. I didn't know about reading the Bible and how it opened a communication with the living God. I didn't know that this book was alive with the Holy Spirit. At age fifteen, I was hungry for love and attention and encouragement. That age for me, like so many others, was the pivotal point for decision-making. I thought at age fifteen I was capable of making life-changing decisions. Unfortunately, our cognitive development plays a cruel trick on us that mature part of our brain is hidden until several years to come.

I dated a few boys. It was always the same. The first boy I connected with was four years older. He was the first to say he loved me. I fought to stay with him. I thought he was the only one who would ever love me. I was not capable of attracting any other. I felt homely, stupid, and lucky that anyone would pay attention to me. Throughout my childhood, there had been little digs here and there, and having an older sister to validate them didn't help me. Perhaps they were just joking remarks, but they rooted in the deepest part of my heart, and I believed every one of them.

Is there something you believe about yourself that is hurtful to you? Does it make you feel like less of a person? Is it really the truth? You can change this. Now I know what we perceive as true *we actually make true* when we allow it to have power over who we are. This is critical to understand. Life and death are truly in the tongue, as the Bible says. When we speak positive things to ourselves, the spirit becomes empowered and lifted up and the flesh must obey it.

The flesh is weak and is controlled by what and where we allow our thoughts to take us. Now I know not to claim negative things that may be said of me or at me. Now I know that they can be warded off. Speak what you want to see happen, "I am healthy, I am beautiful, I am smart" when you say "I will never lose weight", or iI feel like I am going to be sick" you are giving the body permission to do just that. STOP IT.

We must refuse to accept this destruction to our very being. We must remember who we are. We are made in the image and likeness of the Holy One who created us. We must also remember to live by this as well. That means not to return insult or evil, God explained in His Word that we must bless those who speak against us or we will miss His blessing. I urge you to speak good and positive things into your life and over your loved ones. You will see the change all around you as this becomes evident. I am learning to continue to practice this, and I must confess I have found peace in doing so. **Do not be deceived**.

Wordly Lies

Society's perception controls your status as a person. Society said that you had to be beautiful to be important or to succeed. I was a far cry from that, or so I thought. Society said sex was great; important men put their whole life on the line for it –the movies, the TV, all reiterated the same thing.

I had to keep this relationship no matter what. It was the only relationship that allowed me to feel loved. I was afraid, but I did whatever was necessary to keep this boy, even becoming accustomed to alcohol. It was part of every date, like a parasite, keeping me weak, numb. I just went along with it all. When I succumbed to his demands, it was not with consent but out of obligation to this person. If not, he threatened to leave me. I felt betrayed; it was all a lie! No one said how awful this act really was! How violated it made me feel, how painful; this made me feel even worse about myself, my worth, and my value as a person was evaporating more and more. How could they lie to us? I wondered, *Where was God? Why am I alive? What is life all about?* The one person I believed and lived for hurt me. Now I questioned, *why do I feel so bad, isolated, and used? But he was the only one,* I thought, *who could ever love me.*

I persisted until my dad allowed me to get married. I was a junior in high school. Nothing else mattered. My mother never agreed; she had me talk to counselors, but my ears were closed, I thought no one understood my life. How wrong I was. All it would have taken was five words from my mom or dad, "I love you. Stay home", They were never spoken. I left home, and one week after my sixteenth birthday, we were married by a Justice of the Peace. Needless to say, I had no idea what I was getting in to or what was really going on.

I became pregnant right away. I was sick for weeks with morning sickness that lasted all day long. I seemed to put myself into such a state of mind that I would still be able to live a different life someday. I was committed to carrying out what I started to avoid my mom's "I told you so's". I thought this suffering would save my wretched soul, help me get into heaven, and spend less time burning in purgatory. I prayed all the prayers I learned as a child –each one had indulgences, or points, that went toward your time spent in purgatory. I questioned why a loving God would make an imperfect human being, knowing he would fail, just to punish him when he did. Is this the God I want to know? I missed my family terribly, but I had to keep this pain inside for fear of repercussions, and I could not bear to let my mom know she was right. I was in a bad situation.

My husband would purchase alcohol for minor's and they would come over and drink at the little house we lived it. It was not unusual for a fight to break out. I hated it. I saw no future, and I worried about my unborn baby. I didn't dare tell anyone about how we were living. My husband helped his dad so we could put food on the table because his little plant was on strike. I yearned for my parents and younger brothers, but when I cried, I was told I was nothing but a big baby, like my mother said. My husband knew how to manipulate me. I felt broken in many ways. I did not attend church, nor did I have anyone to talk to about what I was going through. I was angry about the things I was taught because I was living in a prison. I had contempt for myself. My thoughts of my little baby gave me comfort but were also a source of worry about his or her future as well. I did not realize my mother would have forgave me and allowed me to come home. Pride and horrible guilt held me in bondage.

Bondage

My world was small. It was too late. I would dream about my family I left and wake up with tears streaming down my face. I knew I couldn't go back. I was not allowed to drive. I had to have permission to call them. I even fibbed to my mom and told her we had our marriage blessed by a Catholic priest in a nearby town so she would stop writing me letters of condemnation. Because our marriage was performed by a Justice, I believed I was doomed (as Mom said) to hell. I felt so worthless, hopeless. My baby was the only thing that gave me a reason to live. I would talk to the child, sing. I bought a baby book and kept a journal in it.

My young husband got a job on a dairy farm, so we moved there. We had much better income, with free meat and milk too. We lived in a twenty-six-foot trailer that was eight feet wide. The small heater by the door had a problem that is someone touched the handle of the door, they would get a shock. Needless to say, it kept me inside most of the time. I had to go to the main house basement to get a shower. The boss and his wife were very good to us. My husband was always getting animals to try to make money, and I had to feed them. A person hasn't lived until they try to teach a calf how to drink milk from a bucket. We had a chicken coop too. I learned how to plant some vegetables and keep a garden, and cooking was by trial and error. One day my husband came in the trailer with a pheasant in his pant leg, he pulled it out and demanded

I clean it up for his supper. I had never done it before, but I had watched him do it. I did the best I could and luckily prepared it to his satisfaction. Necessity truly is the mother of invention —so is fear!

We spent every Sunday up at my husband's parents'. Even when there were road hazards out, we had to go there. I was not able to go see my parents. I spent most of my time out of doors when I could. I loved the big farmland and the beauty of the country. My world was pretty small and very lonely.

I was isolated. I didn't have a driver's license. I felt I couldn't finish school. I tried praying for help the way the Catholic education taught me. Nothing was happening. I prayed for God to show me the truth. There were so many different ideas about religion and God. I needed answers. I just kept on going with the daily expectations.

When I was five months pregnant, the physical abuse from my spouse began. I was knocked down because I was not watching his beagle dog that was in heat close enough. He wanted purebred puppies. He made it clear when he spoke that I was to pay attention. I had no recourse but to continue down this road. I felt I was being duly punished for my sins of immorality. I prayed the rosary but feel into depression that held me in a pit of rebellion, anger, loneliness, and hopelessness, yet I pretended all was well to everyone, even my family. I still felt God's presence, but only as my judge and jury. I just felt that life seemed so unfair.

Why wasn't God listening? Have you ever felt confined, that there was no way out? Did you ever feel that you exhausted all your options? Do you ever want to give up like I did? There is something that can be done.

An Open Door

I had no idea what was ahead of me –so many locked doors and so many things involved. I befriended the mother of one of the boys who worked on the farm we lived on. She was a Protestant and played the organ at a local church. She listened to me and gave me sincere advice and became a close friend. She was an instrument in my first step to peace. So many things she taught me were foreign to me, but she went through the Bible and showed me what it said. I attended the same local Protestant church where she played the organ, and joined the choir she led. She inspired me and encouraged me. This gave me a path to follow and opened the door to the truth.

Even though I attempted to find truth and solace in church. I became more depressed over the years with continues physical, emotional abuse and pregnancies. I still experienced that doomed feeling I has as a child.

When I was twenty-four, I had this strong feeling of doom again, and three days later my sister-in-law lied at age twenty-six. This happened again in the same year. I told my husband, "someone I love is going to die". I was up all night just beside myself. I thought it was someone in my family, but it was a friend who was found dead from a hunting accident.

Before my father died, I felt it again; I wrote him a letter, but he was gone before he received it. I had just given birth to my fourth child a few days before. This loss was really difficult for me. I thought of dying. I needed any release from this emotional pain, which was deeper than an abyss. The blackness enfolded me like a cloak. I was unable to get beyond my pain. I would hold my precious children close, and I would weep from loneliness. I searched for truth.

My Protestant lady friend told me to read the Bible. I began with the New Testament and finally broke away from the indoctrination I suffered as a child. I continued reading the Bible and cried out from the depths of my soul. I found that I didn't have to pay for my sins after all. Jesus did it for me! He loves me *just* as I am. I am forgiven when I acknowledge that He is my Savior, and although I knew of Him, I did not know how to get salvation up to that point. I had given my life to Go and gave each of my children to Him as well. I totally repented and gave Him my life again. I began to love my Lord instead of just fearing him. I knew He was a just God, but what He did for me was beyond human understanding.

I heard, "Love the sinner and hate the sin." But guilt kept creeping in my mind and spirit—guilt from not practicing Catholicism (my mom and sister often reminded me). I called myself a Christian and had to live my faith, not a religion. Guilt still held me. I had to get approval from someone.

I made an appointment with a nun from a Catholic parish not far from where I lived. I explained how I loved god and how I wanted to serve Him. I also told her of the physical and emotional torment I was living in—how I thought I was paying for my past sins. She explained how God loves me and had a purpose for my life and that I was being a self-made martyr by continuing in this marriage. God did not want to see me waste my energies but to put them forth for His Will and serve Him. This woman gave me new insight and understanding of my Lord and Savior. She helped me understand that I had worth to the Master of the universe. This took a long time to digest. Why would I matter to God? I kept slipping back, moving ahead, and slipping again. I had to look forward, yet I felt like a rubber band held me each time I tried to break away, pulling me.

I began to learn and search and pray for daily guidance from my Jesus, and He began to bring me out of the depths of despair. I put my life in His hands. It was the beginning of change. And He is there for you too.

Rebirth

I just dedicated myself to serving Jesus Christ in all I did. This would either be as a wife and mother or wherever He would lead me. I met hard resistance from my husband, but I had a new boldness to succeed. I still fell; sometimes it was easier to drink and forget, but I could not let my children have a mother like that I kept telling myself I could do this with God's help. I would ask forgiveness and keep taking one small step at a time.

One step I had to accomplish was getting my GED and find a job. I made arrangements to take the GED. At age twenty-five I completed my GED with high scores after my third child was born. I had tried hiding birth control methods over the years, but my husband would ask me if I was taking anything to prevent pregnancy, and I couldn't lie. Then he would punish me. I was carrying out fifth child while we were being sustained financially with the help of social services I quite working as aide in my third trimester as the job required heavy lifting I no longer could do. I continued talking to God and making mistakes in my life while hoping for a better tomorrow.

You see, growing close to Jesus doesn't mean you will never fail or fall or take a few or several, steps backward. He knows who we are –He made us. He knows what we need to improve and keep going forward. As we continue to strive to know Him better and get a deeper relationship with Him, we begin backsliding less and less.

I was blessed that at the time, the governor had instituted programs to assist people on welfare to get a skill and break the government-dependent cycle. I took examinations that determined what program would be best suited for me. I was planning on going to school for the year LPN program so I could take care of my children. I waited patiently in prayer for the testing results. I told the Lord I wanted to do His Will. I prayed that I didn't want to make any decisions on my own. If He wanted me to stay in the same rut, I would do it with praise to Him.

I was so full of intense feelings of ambiguity after trying to reason with my husband, that I punched out the window in the garage after being up for three nights. I thought I was having a nervous breakdown. The glass split my wrist open, I was carrying my fifth child and I had to drive myself to the doctor for sutures. My husband wasn't going to be bothered. I prayed, I waited, and one night, at eight months pregnant with this child, after being in the barn with the horses, I fell on my knees in despair and begged for an answer. I cried out, "Why have you forsaken me?" As soon as I heard this come forth from my mouth, I immediately realized, *Jesus knew; Jesus knows.*

On the cross as He hung, He too cried out the same words. The next day, I received the news. I was told my education would be paid for. I would be enrolled at a local college for the RN program and get a stipend each week for gas. I would start in the Fall after my baby was born. I felt joyful of the prospects of the future.

I still had to have the baby and get prepared. That was not easy as I thought. I passed the due date by over four weeks. I was in and out of labor. When the bleeding started, I called the doctor and was put in the hospital. The birth was manual. My doctor told me not to get pregnant again; It was too close for comfort. The baby and I were nearly lost.

I struggled with getting a tubal ligation at age thirty prior to starting school. The old adage that a woman was made for having babies stuck in my head. My mother never knew about this; she believed people who did this were committing a horrible sin. I cried and prayed for days before seeing a doctor. I asked the Lord to help me do what He wanted for me.

One night while I slept, I had a vivid encounter. I was pulled upward, like the feeling of falling in a dream, only in reverse, and *whoosh,* upward I went. I looked into the most beautiful deep-sea blue eyes, as if I were looking into the ocean depths. I saw nothing else but the eyes, yet He was there. It seemed that there was no end to Him; it was as though He absorbed my very being. I was spellbound by His eyes. No words were spoken, but an understanding came over me; I knew I could stop having children and go on with God's plan for my life. I cannot put into words the feeling of freedom, newness, and joy I felt. I was ready to step forward. I knew it would be a struggle. I knew this would be the beginning of the rest of my life for Jesus. I went against my husband's wished and had the tubal ligation surgery.

Two weeks later, I began my college education: five days a week, eight hours a day, and fifteen credits for the next two semesters. The first day of class, my car died a block away from the college. I just prayed that the devil could not thwart what God had planned for me.

A full schedule of classes and five children at home left little time for sleep. It was difficult with a new baby, an alcoholic husband, and four other children who needed love and attention too. I told God I would study and that He would be the One to get me through it. I could not do it without Him. I prayed and cried every day for the next three years.

This course required an 80 percent passing grade. It was a constant struggle because my husband did not want me to succeed. He had started school before I did, and I was doing some of his schoolwork too to help him so he could also finish and be a lab technician; this way we would always have a job in the medical field. He failed three times, as he did not complete his studies because he drank daily. I wrote all his English papers, even while I was in the hospital after I had the baby. I told him he had to do his history himself. I nearly failed too during my last year in school when I drank too much alcohol the night before my

OB exam. My husband made me go with him to a party instead of studying, and I just wanted to forget it all, it was so hard. I was so weak. I was totally controlled by fear of him. People who have never experienced this in their life cannot understand how a person can be so controlled.

A DIVINE APPOINTMENT

The next day, hungover, I took the exam. It was only by the grace of God that I made it through the test with a passing grade. I was so ashamed and felt like such an idiot. I had one supporter; my oldest daughter. She was only thirteen but mature beyond her years. She encouraged me and told me, "Dad wants you to quit. Mom, You can do this". She was my right-hand girl—I praise God for giving me my wonderful children. They gave me the reason to go on. I surely would have committed suicide if I would not have had the children. I came close more than once. God knew this. So among my studies, I made it a point to study about alcohol abuse, family dynamics and addictions.

After three hard years, I graduated with honors, and my three-year-old daughter walked with me in my nursing candlelight pinning service. This was just the beginning of what God had planned for me. He promises to be with us. But we have to work; it is not just done for us. We have to take the next step, knowing that he works through us, for us. It is sometimes grueling, but He never fails us. He holds us, but we must still move forward –one step, one day, right now. I learned I am nothing; I can do nothing without Him. He lifted me up and brought be forth and game me life!

I graduated, and my husband was home drunk. I knew he felt threatened because now I could take care of the family on my own. He never understood my faith and called me names and threatened me when I talked about Jesus to his friends. My heart ached, and I wanted relief. I had left several times before my education but always came back because I knew I couldn't take care of the kids alone. Now that I had my degree, I still thought that if God wanted this relationship to continue, I would keep trying.

Reconciliation

I wanted things to improve in our marriage for the sake of the children. Every time I talked to my husband about Jesus, he would get mad and call me a "Bible thumper". I told him I could not live the life he was living. Barhopping was his favorite pastime. He was into perverted sexual practices and brought materials into the house that were appalling to me. I was afraid for my daughters. I filed for divorce after much prayer. I told my husband he could stay if he was willing to go to AA (Alcoholics Anonymous) and go to church. He agreed.

Two weeks before the divorce became final, I dropped the case. I believed everyone deserved a second chance. I told him I felt nothing and that I didn't hate him but I didn't feel love either. I was numb. I loved my nursing, and found out he was spending my check before I got paid and charging groceries when I gave him money to pay for them. He would go to the bar and spend the cash there.

By the Fall, I filed for divorce again; this time I told him he had to leave. He had slapped my oldest daughter in the face when the kids came running down the stairs after hearing me scream while he was knocking me around. He flung up the stairway door and started swinging. That was the last straw for me. He either did not discipline or he over-disciplined. There were several situations the children endured as a result of his decisions to punish, and I was too passive to argue with him. I was afraid to. I learned from my nursing education how damaging this was for the children. Unfortunately, significant emotional damage was already done, as my older children were fourteen, seventeen and eighteen at the time of separation. Many of their decisions reflected this after they left home. Reconciliation was attempted on more than one occasion, but he would not change and said I was the one with the problem. He said he was happy living the way he was. He tried to talk me into changing my mind, and when I would not go with him, he became very angry and threatening. That is when I told him I was sorry; he really did not know me after all these years we had been together if he could treat me like that. I knew I made the right decision to separate when he showed his true colors. I submerged myself into my Lord, my children and my work.

I worked afternoon shifts at the hospital. While I was there, my estranged husband would come to the house and take things, even my medication. He would convince the children I was the problem. When the kids would call me and tell me he was there, I would get physically ill. One afternoon I had chest pains and had to be admitted to the ICU unit for observation. My estranged husband came down to the hospital and brought my older daughter, and took my car. He was continually trying to manipulate me so I would let him back. I had problems with the furnace in the old house. I just kept saying, "Lord, tomorrow will be better, I trust you". I kept a diary this time and wrote everything down that I was going through and how I felt. By reading this, I would recall how he worked me. It was extremely stressful as I had to deal with the emotions of all the children, as well as my own. It was only by the grace of God I was able to follow through until we were legally divorced. I am not saying divorce is the answer to marital problems. This was only after consulting with professionals and ultimately with my Lord, who led me to freedom.

Liberty

I never knew freedom. Once my husband was out of the house, I felt such relief. I didn't have to worry about what he would be doing when I got home from work. It was as though a heavy yoke was removed from my neck. I was not really happy, just relieved. I felt free to be myself. The chains were broken! Not many people knew what I had gone through. My husband had his bar friends, and a lot of lies about why I filed for divorce were being spread around the little town. I didn't want the children to know why either; no sense to hurt them because this man was still their father. God knew, and I knew the truth, that is all that mattered. I knew I could count on the Lord to take me down the path He wanted for me. I still made mistakes, but His mercies are new every day.

 Giving your life to Jesus doesn't mean you won't make mistakes or that you will always do things right. It makes you more aware of when you do make poor decisions. It is as though your conscience becomes more alive when the Holy Spirit is allowed to be in control. This Spirit gives a freedom that leaves you wanting more. There is plenty to go around for the asking.

 No matter where we are in life, there is nothing like the peace God can give you. We each have a path to follow Every person has pain, disappointments, sometimes despair. Every person has a story to tell. I

 pray you will allow yourself to know the living God who created you. He is the path to peace. He is the liberation you desire. When you are boxed in and feel like there is nothing left, take it to Him.

He will give you completeness, liberty, and joy. It is okay to fall, but not okay to stay there. God will give you grace to go on, one step at a time. Then when you finally can see the journey you have taken, you can look back and smile and say, "Yes, He truly held my hand and led me through the fire and trials. I let go but He did not. "Praise Him for His faithfulness.

Trusting

I grew up dependent. Then I was dependent on my husband. Through that relationship, I was taught to be independent. I had to learn to assert myself and educate myself. Now it was time to become dependent on Jesus Christ. This was a process and not easy to do. It took time, but this is what faith is all about.

I talked to God constantly. He says in His Word to ask. We cannot receive without asking. He says in His Word to pray as it has been answered for you already. To just *know* that out of love it is done. He has done it. It began with little things. One instance when I was waiting for approval for my daughter's college funds. On Friday, I said, "Lord I know you will come through on this." The check came on the following Monday. Every time something else would break down in the house, I would just tell Him, "I know tomorrow will be better."

I read in the Bible that the power of life and death is in the tongue. When we say positive and encouraging things, it brings about things that are good, including good health. When we say negative things or think them the results are discontent and discouragement. The Bible says what a man thinks so shall he be. Words matter.

We establish how we speak throughout our lifetime. It becomes habitual. Change has to first be a desire, and then we must *purposefully* act on it one day at a time. This is one of the most important aspects of trusting. Know that when you expect great things, He will give you great things. God was not through with me and was teaching me, and I was willing.

A DIVINE APPOINTMENT

Many times at work, I would have a client who was difficult to put an IV line in. I would say, "Lord this one is yours. They need this medication, and they need it now. Guide my hands and get this in". It worked every time. I always gave Him the credit and the glory. I would tell the other nurses how it happened when they asked. I told them Jesus did it for me. I loved my hospital nursing and all my clients. They taught me to appreciate my abilities and my health.

I met many courageous and loving folks. One man thought he had the big "C" (cancer). He said he was going to be "worm meat". I said, "Do you really believe that?" I told him that God loved him and that God told me he didn't have cancer. He said if that happened with the testing the following day, he would seriously rethink his philosophy and change his attitude. I was off work a few days, and when I came back I was met at his door with a big hug. He said he didn't have cancer after all and he would never forget our little talk.

God put people in my care who taught me about Him. I had a client whose body was so riddled with arthritis we could not move her without her screaming in pain. She wondered why she was not able to die. I was amazed at her courage to go on each day. Her family loved her greatly, and she was an obvious inspiration to them. I told her she still was giving to those around her, including me. I did not understand why I was the caregiver and she was the patient. I often wondered if I could tolerate the suffering I saw on a daily basis and put it in His hands like many of my patients did.

God spoke to me often when I was at work, alerting me to the needs of others who were in my care. I am ever grateful for every client that I had the privilege to serve. I learned so much from each and every one of them, and I loved and prayed for all of them.

Another Step

My future was uncertain. One night on the way back to my car in the parking structure, I twisted my ankle and broke it. I didn't realize it was broken. I drove to a coworker's house in town, put ice on it and elevated it. After an hour, I drove the thirty miles home, using my left foot. Normally I would have been driving about fifty-five miles an hour, but because of my ankle, I was driving much slower. I suddenly came onto a huge group of deer right in the middle of the road and was able to stop safely. The ankle had a lot of swelling and pain when I got home. I went to bed and elevated it on a pillow with ice and an ace wrap.

I went to work the next day but ended up in the emergency room when I couldn't stand walking on it. It was put in a cast. I had to be off work for a while.

This happened just a few days before my flight to Texas. I knew it was not God's plan, but I had gone anyway, and it was wrong. I had dated a coworker's brother who moved to Texas, and he told me it was cheap living down there. I planned on going for a visit to check it out. I really was not thinking. This person was a recovered alcoholic, and it wasn't until I saw him in Texas that I realized he was just like the man I had divorced in too many ways. I came home early. It was a horrible plane trip. Lightening storms cause the plane to pitch and drop. I prayed all the way home, asking for forgiveness for going. When I arrived home I thanked God and once again promised to improve my behavior. I told God I didn't need another man to be happy. I had five kids to consider and take care of. I told God that if

A DIVINE APPOINTMENT

He had someone He wanted in my life to send him to me; I was not looking. I had to lean on Jesus, not another earthly man. I had no idea what God had in mind.

Six weeks later, I had the cast removed. I was out walking to strengthen my leg, as the calf was much smaller that the other leg. When I returned home, my children told me a man was at the house and wanted to ask me out for a date. I never knew this man. He lived just a few miles away, and his younger daughter was friends with my youngest daughter. He also knew my best girl friend. He called and made a blind date with me. He had two little girls, and his ex-wife was living out of state. He went to church and seem like a nice person. Little did I know that this first date would culminate in a marriage after just three months. We had so many things in common. First, Jesus was number one. Each time we were together, more and more compatible factors were revealed. Even silly little things! I had the iron, and he had the ironing board. I had a salt and pepper shaker of two children on their knees praying. I accidentally broke one of them. When I went to his house, he had the one I had broken. After we were married, they were a set again.

In just a few weeks of dating, he said he wanted to marry me, that he would wait until I was ready, and that he knew this was ordained by God. I was gun-shy. Marriage was a scary move for me, but through prayer and many events, I knew it was the right thing to do. I prayed and talked to older, wiser women. In my heart I knew this man was different. That is, when I let myself fall, and I fell in love with his children too in a matter of days. They were so hungry for a mother's love, and I had plenty to give. They never understood why. We were married, and the girls were in the wedding. It took about six months for them to realize having a mom didn't change the love their daddy had for them. I told them it was like putting an extra blanket on when you are cold. I could never take their mom's place.

The kids had become a family. I was "Mom Jan" and was very protective of these little girls. Things seemed to move along well, with the exception of a lot of interference from the ex-spouses who even conspired together. These people constantly indoctrinated the children against us. Three years after our wedding, our two girls ended up going to live with their biological mom. We fought the good fight with the court but put it in God's hands and knew that whatever happened, they would be all right because God would take care of them. The case was never resolved in court. The judges were changed, the ex's lawyer was his friend, the "friend of the court" just said he was recommended the children go no matter what. We were railroaded in to signing papers to let them go. We both grieved for weeks. Working with the court system

With two ex-spouses is a nightmare (I could write another book about it). It was only through our love, prayer and the grace of God that we got through all the stress.

A Bump In The Road

We never know what tomorrow brings. Four years after we were married, we put the old house up for sale. There were multiple reasons: y sons were getting involved in activities we did not approve of. I had to get them away from some bad influences. My husband was working over an hour away; I worked a half hour away and was traveling over an hour to college for my Bachelor's in Nursing. The house sold in one week. We found a small ranch house right where we needed to be.

A few weeks later, while working in the hospital I sustained a spinal injury. It ended my hospital career. I was in constant pain. I was unable to take pain medication. It made me very sick and I didn't like how it made my head feel. My husband had to take over all the household chores with the children. I did what I could but was very restricted. This put a real strain on the relationships with my stepdaughters too.

This injury resulted in three surgeries over two years in attempt to correct the problems. The first surgery was an outpatient procedure. Although I was anesthetized, I was awake. I was taped down on my side and a large trocar was inserted into the spinal area, validated by continual X-ray monitoring. The disc material was removed, and after a few hours I was sent home. I lay in the backseat, and we drove the ninety miles home. Early the next morning, I broke out in hives, and my head was whirling. I had to go to the emergency room, where I was diagnosed with an allergic reaction from the medications that were given to me during the surgery. It took weeks for the vertigo to diminish. However, the vertigo returned whenever I tried any medication for pain, including aspirin. I had to use ice and just lie on my back for relief.

Two years later I had another surgery where I spent a few days in the hospital. My recovery was slow, and I still had problems. After the third surgery, I seemed a little better. During that time we traveled to Niagara Falls: I had an aunt who resided near there. After we arrived, we were having breakfast, and I had that feeling of doom. I told my husband we needed to pay for protection over our children, so we did. At 5:00 p.m, we called the children from the hospital from the hotel. Our youngest son had been involved in single rollover car accident. The vehicle rolled three times, and it was full of teenagers. None of them were hurt, with the exception of one girl who had some glass shards in her knee. We praised the Lord for being faithful. He is always listening. Just talk to Him. He wants you to "bother" him. He *loves* it. I challenge you to ask and be open to receive. You will be blown away with the results. God's love is so intense and immeasurable. Believe and receive. I can assure you, and let me tell you why.

The Waiting Room

An unforeseen experience was about to occur. I was hoping, as I turned forty, that I would start menopause and wouldn't have to put up with the painful monthly curse. I only had five days without pain each month. I would toss and turn and cry and roll. I hated the thought of surgery and hoped it would just go away. Denial is so easy.

My husband insisted that I go to a physician, and fibroid tumors were discovered. I was attending college four days a week so I set the surgery up over Christmas break. The surgery was horrific. In the recovery room I was conscious but couldn't open my eyes. I heard my doctor say, "I am worried about her kidney function, so do a fluid challenge". That means they run IV fluids in rapidly to get the kidneys to respond. When I woke up, I was told the tumors were so large that they had worked all the way back to the spine. My doctor said that the inside of my abdomen looked like hamburger. They took the uterus and ovaries, as they were abnormal too. I had a large vertical abdominal incision as a result.

I went home and tried to recover. I kept feeling little stinging feelings in my belly. I thought they were adhesions popping. On New Year's Eve, I had "that feeling"; it was overwhelmingly strong. I called my adult children and warned them not to drink and drive. They know how this works. I went to bed, praying protection over all of them.

Little did I know what was going to happen. I was dreaming I was having my monthly in bed. I awoke at 4:00 a.m. hemorrhaging vaginally. I had abdominal surgery. I knew I was in trouble. A sudden rush of fear came over me.

Then I said to myself, "This is the day you meet your Maker. This is what you are taught all your life, so be at peace." I began to pray the Psalm 23 (KJV):

The Lord is my shepherd: I shall not want. He maketh me to lie down in green pastures; He leadeth me beside the still waters. He restoreth my soul; He leadeth me in paths of righteousness for His name's sake. Yea, though I walk through the valley of the shadow of death, I will fear no evil; for thy rod and thy staff they comfort me. Thou preparest a table before me in the presence of mine enemies; thou anointest my head with oil; my cup runneth over. Surely goodness and mercy shall follow me all the days of my life; and I will dwell in the house of the Lord for ever.

I dialed 911. I knew I could not survive long while bleeding so heavily. I hated to wake up my husband, but I knew I had to. I called a local physician who had an office four miles from our home. I told him what was happening. I told him I needed an IV to keep from going in to shock.

I put myself head-down in the backseat of the car, and my husband drove up to the doctor's office. The doctor started the large bore IV in my left arm and said it looked like the bleeding had clotted off. The ambulance picked me up from there. It was New Year's Day, and there were road warnings out, as well as freezing rain and ice. They took me to a hospital twenty-five miles away. My husband and youngest daughter drove our car. They beat the ambulance. I could still feel the little bee stings in my abdomen.

I was in the emergency room for many hours. I had IV blood running in each arm and one in my right jugular vein in my neck. My doctor who did the surgery was not on call. I had a resident who failed to notify the surgeon who *was* on call. I had no pain. I really wasn't thinking too clearly. I had blood draws every half hour it seemed. I was very pale; even my lips were white. I kept praying and speaking to the Lord.

The emergency doctor decided to move me to a bed in the hospital. I asked for the obstetric floor as I had a friend who worked there. She was off that day, as were the surgical teams, since it was a holiday. When I was pulled off the gurney onto the hospital bed on the obstetrics floor, I felt a 'pop' inside my abdomen. I didn't know it was the uterine artery suture letting loose. That did it. My life was draining away. I was on oxygen, and my head was lower than my feet to preserve the organs and brain.

The supervising nurse came in and lifted the sheet and ran out and got the ball rolling. Soon, the surgeon who was on call was in the room, an OR team was setting up, and my bed was pushed into the operating room.

My husband and ten-year-old daughter were in the corner of the room crying when I rolled by. I was pulled onto the OR table, and a mask was put over my face. I thought that was it. I kept praying and waited for the familiar garlic taste of the medication that is given to put you under, before losing consciousness. I was beginning to have trouble breathing, and suddenly, blackness. Then I woke up.

I was shouting, "I'm alive! I'm alive!" I found myself totally in another place. I could see and hear and feel. I was surrounded by a bright fog, and a black tunnel was to my upper left.

A man's voice said, "You have to go back. You have work to do". I felt so free and wonderful. I could feel this overwhelming love envelope me —a love I cannot define without weeping. I can only say that when you feel Him holding you, you understand how He really does know every hair on your head, every heart ache. He really cares about each and every one of us. How? I don't have to know that anymore. I just know we have so much to gain with loving Jesus. He feels every pain of every one of us. He wants all of us to be with Him. He wants a *relationship*. He weeps over our sins but told me it is more hurtful when we do not meet the needs of others —the sins of omission. He said that time is short and that He wants his people to know how much He loves them.

Then I began hearing noises and seeing swirling methodical colors in my head: *chunk, chunk, chunk,* almost like a pinwheel and then tumbling blocks—thirty years and I still recall it vividly. I began to think, *what happened?* I regained consciousness but was not "awake"; I felt heavy, as though I was buried under wet sand. I told myself that I had an out- of- the body experience! I wanted to get out and feel that free again. I wept. I prayed. I said, "Now I know the burdens we carry in this flesh –heavy, heavy, burdens". I had revelations flooding into my mind. I felt so euphoric.

I said to myself, "I never thought of who I was or where I was, just that *I was, I am –as God told Moses, tell my people I am.* I never thought of being a nurse, a mom, a wife, a sister, just that I *was* – the whole meaning of a life –you *are* and God *is.* I never thought of taking a breath, yet I felt more alive and free than I have ever experienced.

I looked around yet I could not see my hands or my body. Actually, at the time, I didn't even think of having one. I heard, "You must go back. You have work to do", as plain as day. For weeks I was afraid I would not be able to fulfill His work. I prayed that I wouldn't let Him down and that He would give me what I need each step of the way. I knew then that pain I had gone through was fleeting, between God and me. When you leave this body, pain is over, gone, like it never happened. I prayed that whatever reason there is for pain, it is okay with me. I know what is waiting for me. I said to the Lord, "I will take it gladly in Your name". Pain is gone, this world is gone –you step into a new realm. It is indescribable, and I was only in the waiting room!

The Sign

God has a way of getting our attention. When we realize that God is just a breath away, anything is possible. He is there to help you continue. When you are in pain, and when you feel you have no hope, focus on your relationship with Jesus instead, and wonderful things will happen. I had five major surgeries while attending college for my Bachelor's degree in nursing. I knew my spinal problems limited my nursing options and that career opportunities would significantly improve with advancement of my education. It is only because I depended on God to get me through that I succeed in anything. Each day I thought it would be easier to just quit. But I could not go backward. I had to take each day, each hour and keep going. I carried a pillow to school and a soft lawn chair to get through lectures. I knew without my advanced degree, my options for employment would be minimal. I knew God would lead me. I give Him *all* the praise, for I can do nothing on my own. That is what surrender means; know He wants you to ask. He wants to give you all the good things available – these things are waiting for you if you *ask* and are willing to listen softly to His urgings. When you get tired of trying to fix it all yourself, He is there, waiting. I am so thankful He did not give up on me. He would gently urge me in my very being to do things; however, sometimes, His communication was not so subtle.

God has a sense of humor. I was driving ninety miles to the hospital for my job while recuperating with the spinal problem. I was on worker's compensation so I had to drive the ninety miles four days a week. I left early in the morning and drove east. I usually had a beautiful sunrise or saw some wildlife on the way. One dreary morning, I was just a few miles from town when the thought flashed in to my mind: *Lord, you didn't send me any beauty this morning – no sunrise, no deer.* Instantly a large rooster pheasant flew right in front of my face beyond the windshield, inches away, it came out of nowhere! My leart leapt into my throat, and then I laughed and said, "Oh, you are funny, aren't you Lord?"

After that day, many times when I was feeling low or worrying about something in my life, forgetting to focus on God and not my problems, I would turn a corner and there would be a large rooster pheasant strutting his stuff just for me. It was as though God was reminding me that He was still taking care of things for me. My job is to remember that He is faithful and to focus on Him first. It never failed. I would smile and say, "Yes, thank you. I know you are still there. Even though I am not worthy, your are faithful". The rooster pheasant had become a very special sign to me. This beautiful, colorful male bird will pop up out of no where when I am focusing on my own feelings, heartache, or pain. This reminds me where the focus must be: on Jesus. He has my back.

The Power Of Prayer

Through the years, I learned many prayers of the Catholic Church by memorization, and then I learned prayer meant just *talk* to the Lord. I would pray from down deep in my heart. Prayer is not something that is hard –it is any communication we have with our Lord. He *loves* to hear from you. He *wants* to show you how much your are loved. You can communicate all feelings to Him: anger, pain, doubt. He will allay all of them for you, if you allow Him to come in and be your Savior. He must be invited; He will not force you. You can challenge Him. He doesn't have to answer, but He does. He tries to get our attention, and sometimes, through our poor choices, we face a crisis and then cry out to Him. You need to be ready when this happens. You have to surrender your own will and let Him lead. When you learn that you *can* trust Him explicitly, you will keep walking one foot in front of another and feel the love surround you as you journey along. Be excited how He will change your life and bring you peace. Yes, you may fail. Yes, you may get frustrated, but hand on. Someone is holding you and will never let you go. Keep going for today and for tomorrow. Know things can and will improve, but we have to be willing to do our part.

Choose His path. The work is to be done in His name. He knows we are not perfect. He created you, remember? He smiles on you and me when we attempt to be obedient. He gets us there. He wants all the blessings and prosperity to be yours. Put your troubles at the bottom of the triangle and God at the top peak. Things will fall into place.

Expect big things from our big God! Often, when we cannot see any way out, something happens. For example, our youngest daughter is married to an army man. He was deployed to Hawaii. This is a primary army station from where the men and women are deployed to Iraq or Afghanistan. While I was praying for protection over my son-in-law, I heard a familiar voice again saying, "He is not going to Iraq".

In my simple bran, I think, *but God…*

You know, we often try to tell God how to do things and give Him advice. So human of us, isn't it? The phrase was repeated: "He is not going to Iraq." I didn't have to know how but just that God would keep my daughter's husband from war. I was overwhelmed with praise and thanksgiving, as they had three children and the baby was only a year old. When I told my daughter, she said she would be fine and that I should not worry; she had faith that God would protect him. I had told her what God had said, and she kind of fluffed if off. My son-in-law did go to desert training. But he sustained an injury to his hearing while on maneuvers prior to the desert training when a flash-bang grenade exploded too close to him. This greatly diminished his ability to hear. He had several doctors look at him and test him. The army reclassified him. My son-in-law loved being an MP and being in the army. But he testified he did not want someone to die because he could successfully communicate or not hear orders. He was retrained in the prison security system and sent back to the States. God knew.

A Time Of Trust

As I have mentioned previously, I have an older sister. After she reached her teen years, it seems all we did was fight. She was my mom's right hand in a lot of ways. I was four years younger, so as life goes, a teenager doesn't want to be bothered by a kid sister. (I suppose I did annoy her purposefully at times). She married a GI a year after she graduated high school and moved away. Four years later, I left home. We had little contact until she was divorced and moved back to the town where my parents live in. She remarried and was happy for ten years, but her husband died from a brain tumor at age fifty. She was devastated. I would go up and visit and call, but we never were close. She lived a lifestyle of drinking and smoking and spent a lot of time in the bars. It was a running joke that she was Mom's favorite. She never let up on condemning me about, as she put it, "Leaving the faith", as she practiced the Catholic religion but not the commandments of god. Don't get me wrong; I am a sinner too. But this was a wedge in our relationship. Every time I tried to teach her about Jesus saving us when He died on the cross and arose, she was not taught that, she would get angry with me, and I would put it aside and pray that God would send her a man who knew Jesus and could help he. God told me that was one reason I was still down here on earth. What? How can I do anything? My sister sank into deep depression. I couldn't get her to come and visit in Florida and spend time with me. At home we were two hours apart.

It had been twenty-four years since her husband died when I felt that doom again. I had been out painting on a small trailer we used to take things to Florida with. My back went in to spasm, and I had to get in the house and grab my ice pack. I could hardly breathe because the spasms were so bad. I took a muscle relaxer and sat in a high back chair and prayed. A few hours later, the nursing home that my mother was in, called and said she had taken a turn for the worse. There was no way I could drive up there. I called my oldest brother, who lived fifteen miles from the home, and he went to check on her. I also let my sister know. Mom lived through the night and passed away the next day. I wasn't able to be with her. I felt such guilt. It was awful.

That Saturday was All Saints Day, appropriate, November 1rst. Mom was so faithful to her Lord and to her church. This was the best day for her to go home and finally see her Lord, along with embracing her twenty-three-year old mother, who died nine days after giving birth to Mom, and her Father, who died the following year from the influenza outbreak 1918, and her beloved first born son and baby girl. No doubt Mom was in heaven.

Usually, after the crisis or person is gone I feel at peace. This time I still had that impending doom feeling. I prayed for my sister. She had been in a lot of pain with her scoliosis and was staying pretty much at home. I made a DVD of Mom's life and left it at the funeral home. When I returned the next day with her clothing, I was told the funeral

Home did not have a player for the DVD. I went to my sister's and spent some time with her. She needed some groceries, so I told her I would go get them, as I had to go out and purchase a small TV and DVD player. I picked up the TV first, and as I stopped at the grocery store, I heard the familiar voice say, "Go to the other store".

I think, *God I didn't know there was another store here.* So I got out of the car and walked around the front of this big grocery store, and sure enough a small furniture shop that rented out their products. I walk in, and they had a big flatscreen TV's in the back. I thought, "*Lord I can't afford to buy one of these things.* I asked the clerk if they had a small TV/DVD player. He said he could order one. The I explained why I needed it. He told me he would set up a nice big TV and DVD at the funeral home for only twenty dollars and that

A DIVINE APPOINTMENT

he would pick it up after the funeral mass. I thanked him, and gave him forty dollars to cover his gas, as it was a fifteen mile trip one way. I then returned the new TV/DVD I had purchased earlier. I felt energized with the Holy Spirit.

I got back to my sister's and told her and she just gave me that 'face'. I spent the night with her. I asked her if I could help her. Her hair was short, and she always ratted it up. It was pretty stiff. She said she had a perm but couldn't give it to herself. She was in too much discomfort. I tried to convince her to allow me to help her, but she would not have any of it –she wasn't up to it. So then I talked her in to just letting me wash her hair for her. She reluctantly allowed that. She lowered her head over the sink, and I washed her hair.

She constantly yelled at me, "You're using too much shampoo," "You're getting me wet," and on and on. She was so negative about everything. I learned to joke with her instead of being hurt. I dried her hair and used a curling iron on it and said, "Now it will be nice for Mom's funeral."

I spent that night at my older brother's. It was hard to be around my sister because she sucked the life out of me. She was so negative. I had to pray and ask God to fill my heart with *His* love so I could give it to her. I didn't seem to have much in my own cup. God always gave me what I needed. I was concerned about her. She did not come to the funeral home for Mom's viewing or the rosary. I stopped to see her that evening. She said that our cousin sent flowers to Mom and that she was supposed to get them. Well, my human nature didn't like that too well. I thought she had some nerve asking for that plant, but that was fine with me if it made her happy.

My niece said that her brother was bringing his mom to the funeral mass. She did not come. Everyone was saying negative things about my sister for not coming. I knew in my heart something was very wrong. My younger son stayed over after the funeral at my brother's with me. The next day, I drove home. I had no contact with my sister. I didn't want to deal with her; I needed time alone. That was on Friday.

After I dropped my son off, I asked God to send me a shooting star so I knew that Mom forgave me for not being there for her, that she knew I loved her, and that she was okay. I popped my Christian worship CD in and continued the hour drive back to my home. I had forgotten my request. I had to stop one mile from my home due to stop sign. I looked up into the sky. There was a bright star that fell straight down, right in front of me –I couldn't miss it. This star was right in the center of my field of vision. I felt a rush of the Spirit come from the bottom of my feet up through my body and out the top of my head. I began to weep with joy.

I prayed, "Thank you, thank you, Lord. I am so unworthy and yet you are so faithful, I love you."

I knew Mom was with Him. When you feel the glory flow through you, you want more; it is such an awesome experience. "Fill my cup, Lord", and He does. Sunday after church, I heard the voice again, *"Go save your sister"*. I told my husband; he knows and accepts when these things happen. We were getting prepared to make our trek to our Florida home for the winter. I didn't let my sister know I was coming.

Monday morning, I packed up the best plant form the funeral home (not the one my cousin sent), mom's rosary, and the cards and things from the funeral service to give to my sister. I left early and stopped and had breakfast on the way up north. I called my sister and asked how she was doing; she literally cried out, "I am waiting for someone to help me!"

I told her I was on my way and prayed God would fill me with what I needed. I arrived, and she was lying on the sofa. She had been spending most of her time in bed. She stood up, and I held her and prayed a healing prayer over her –and she let me! I told her she needed to go to the doctor. She was swearing and cursing. She finally agreed to go to a chiropractor. Her chiropractor was on vacation, so I called the woman whom I had seen on my trips there, she took us right in. My sister went back in the cubicle. The doctor came out and told me my sister was in a lot of pain and couldn't be adjusted. I took my sister back to her home, and she was really mad. I picked up her sweatshirt and checked her abdomen. The liver was hard and swollen and stretched all the way across to the left side of her body. I knew she was in trouble. I could hear her breathing too –fluid in her

A DIVINE APPOINTMENT

lungs. I told her this was the kind of thing people could die from. She told me to shut up, that I was scaring her. I asked her which doctor she wanted to see, and she said she would call someone the next day.

I said, "No, I will call now and take you tomorrow." I told her she should probably go to the emergency room at the hospital, but she didn't have any insurance. She had money put away but didn't want to spend it. She would turn sixty-five in nine weeks and be eligible for Medicare.

She could have bought insurance but chose not to.

She had been going to a nurse practitioner (she wasn't very happy with her), so I called to get her in and took he the next day. My poor sister was in so much pain that she could hardly stand it. She couldn't sit, lay, she could hardly walk. The nurse practitioner told her to go to the hospital. That was not what my sister wanted to hear. She was livid. I called my niece while my sister dressed and told her that her mom was in serious condition and on the way to the emergency room. She met us at the hospital. This was not a good situation. At 11:00 p.m., the doctor dismissed my sister with antibiotics. His diagnosis was slight pneumonia. I told him he was wrong.

"What about the enlarged liver?" I asked. He said it was probably from her chronic drinking. I said, "No, you need to keep her". She didn't want to stay, and I had a log drive home. My sister started to condemn me again, swearing and using God's name in vain. I told her God sent me up there to *save her*. I asked my niece is she would take her mom home, as I decided to make the two hour drive home.

I arrived home after midnight, emotionally exhausted. I kept calling my sister, and she was not getting better. By the third day, I called my niece and told her to take her mom back to the emergency room and demand a CAT scan of the abdomen. She called me back later and said my sister had lung cancer, fourth state. I drove back up to see her. She was pretty mad about the whole thing. At least now she had pain medication.

My niece came over after work, and I got my sister a glass of water. She dropped it; I got her another one, and she dropped that one too. I suspected the cancer had already metastasized to her brain.

I knew then why I had felt that familiar feeling of doom was still there. I left the next day. My niece took a hiatus from work to stay with her mom. My husband and I left for Florida the next day. This was during the third week of November. I had planned on flying back home to be with my sister depending on how she declined. Later that week, my niece brought her mom back to the doctor to see what treatment options they had. They took my sister by ambulance to the city. My niece said they didn't expect my sister to survive the night. This was the weekend before Thanksgiving. I started looking for a flight. I clicked on Monday; God said no. Not until I chose Friday, after Thanksgiving, did He say okay. It was a much higher fare too. On Wednesday, my sister came home on hospice. They set up a hospital bed in the living room, and my niece was staying with her. My sister went into a coma on Thursday. I arrived Friday evening. I thought I was prepared. I walked in and broke down in tears. My niece and nephew were there, as was his wife. We all held hands and prayed. I told her she had to ask Jesus to forgive her, and I also asked her to forgive me. I told her we didn't know how sick she was and avoided her. I told her to ask Jesus to be her Lord. I sat beside my sister and stroked her head. I prayed over her and talked to her. Once in a while she would say "Momma". She could not open her eyes or move.

My niece slept on the sofa next to her mom, and I slept upstairs. In that room was a child's wooden rocking chair. It was given to my mom on her third birthday, September 13, 1920. Mom was ninety-one when she passed over. She had given the chair to my sister years ago, and it always was a sore spot in my heart. You know how that goes. Well, there that chair stood, reminding me that my mom loved my sister and not me. It seemed I had the devil in one ear telling me to put the chair in my truck because my sister could no longer own it. I learned to identify this fleshly sin pusher. I thought, *No you don't. This is about my sister, not you.* I Told my sister that mom loved her so much she couldn't even enjoy heaven without her. I told my sister that e would have that pillow fight again when I got there.

Saturday morning, her breathing became shallow and I knew she would be going home soon. Many visitors had come throughout the day. Our oldest living brother came and sat beside her and wept. This was a man who did not show this kind of emotion. Just after 6:00 p.m., I told my niece to come and sit beside her mom. I sat near her head and held her hand in mine. I kept praying. My sister lifted her fingers up and squeezed my hand three times before she stopped breathing. Her face glowed, and she didn't even look like herself. She was utterly beautiful. I felt the glory enter and take her home. My niece and I held each other and wept I made a joke to myself: *Yeah, she was always first, now first to see Jesus, Mom and Daddy, our brother and sister, cheated again.* I have to admit my spirit was envious but, at the same time, joyous for how God was working in everyone, including me, in the situation. He is like that, you know. Sometimes, when we don't even realize it, He works in us. I knew when I heard the voice say, "Go save your sister". There was more to be done at my sister's house.

Reaching Out

After I had arrived at my sister's, I knew we had a lot of work ahead of us. I told my niece that we should begin packing things up in the apartment, as it had to be vacated. We had the upstairs and much of the living area completed by the time my sister went home with Jesus. I spent the night Sunday at her home. I thought I would leave the basement for the kids to clean out. My back was pretty sore. I went down the stairs and turned the corner at the bottom and said, "Dear Lord, where do I start?" In front of me was a small, glass, three-tiered shelf. It housed shells and coral. The top shelf had a large glass goblet with pieces of coral and shells in it. I dropped to my knees and started wrapping each fragile piece with newspaper and placed it in a box. As I completed the task, I started up the stairs to put them in the kitchen so St. Vincent's de Paul would come and pick up all the stuff by the door. As I started coming up the staircase, I heard the voice again say, "Put them in your truck".

I immediately thought, *I don't need these shells, I go to Florida.*

Then the voice repeated, *"Put them in your truck"*.

I did exactly that –I laid the box in the back of my pickup instead of adding them to the already large amount of things for St. Vincent's de Paul to pick up. I told my niece that evening what had happened. I told her that God had a plan for the sea shells and that He would reveal it later.

Two days later, my niece called me and said, "Uncle Dave called me last night. He wanted to know where the shells went, so I told

A DIVINE APPOINTMENT

him they went to St. Vinny's but that you had the larger ones. He was bummed out about it, as he had given her many of them".

I told her I had them all. I told her not to tell him. God gave me a plan. I went to his home, and it was snowing heavily. I hung a note just inside the door where he could see it as soon as he came through it. It said, "Your journey begins here; follow the footsteps". I had taken all of his shoes I could find and placed them in a walking pattern throughout the house and into his bedroom. Between the shoes was a shell or a piece of coral. God gave me these notes: First, "Every journey begins with one purposeful step"; next, "We may walk as one but we never walk alone"; third, "Even in the darkest, starless night, the Holy Spirit will illuminate your way"; and finally, "Love is like water –it can be cold and hard or wash over you and be gone, or you can breathe it in as a mist and blow it out on those around you". The shoes pointed toward his closed, where I set the large goblet with the remaining coral and shells, along with a three-page letter of what God had communicated to me and completed through that month. I concluded the letter with: "Now you know how much God loves you and how He arranged to give this precious gift." O left feeling great joy in my soul.

I couldn't help but smile as I thought of my brother coming home and finding these things in his house. I had spent the night with my niece and drove home the next day, as my flight was leaving the following day for Florida. I knew my brother would not be home for a few weeks, but I was anxious to hear from him after he did return and find the gift. My brother was not one to keep in close contact, but I knew in God's time, he would call.

As I exited the plane in Florida, I told my husband that I felt so removed from this world with all that happened. It was so euphoric to feel and hear God speak. I felt my feet never touched the ground; it was a surreal feeling. I knew it would be a while before I heard from my brother. I prayed God would speak to his heart, for all I wanted was my family to know and love Jesus as much as I do.

Weeks went by and no contact. Then the call came. He said he came in and saw the note and wondered what the heck was going on. As he read, he said that he was on his hands and knees crawling from one boot to the next; he was laughing and crying at the same time. He said that he couldn't wait to get to the next note. He said he felt very close to our sister and that he would keep those things as long as he lived. I just told him I loved him. He came down to Florida that spring and visited for a few days. He is a deep thinker, and I know Jesus will show him how much he is loved. I look forward to the day he asks Jesus to be his Lord, and one day, we will all be in heaven together. I thanked God for allowing me to be His instrument once again.

Who We Are

We are instruments of the most high place. When we allow the glory of God to enter our body, the temple of the Holy Spirit, the hole only He can fill, then things happen succinctly, precisely, awesomely, smoothly, an supernaturally. When it is completed, the whole experience fills your very soul with such joy. He seems to leave an imprint on our spirit. I cannot fully explain it. Once you experience it, you will thirst for more of it and seek out the opportunity to be the vessel He made us to be. I encourage you to look forward, *not at your problems,* not where your are right now, but where our awesome God wants you to be. He knows you better than you know yourself. When you understand the difference between your carnal desires and your spiritual needs, you will be able to choose more wisely. God is the One who offers you discernment and will create situations to help you learn this. It takes a lifetime. But I tell you, every step is worth it.

You can reach the point when you can look in the mirror and say, "I am not listening to the flesh; My 'self' has an insatiable appetite for sinful things and selfishness, and say, "Thank you, Lord, for showing me what my spirit needs an focusing on you so I do not fall as often." Even though we grow closer to Jesus, we still sin daily –in thought, word, or deed. Sometimes it jus seems to be 'there' in the mind and you don't know where they came from, say, "Be gone in the name of Jesus. Lord fill my mind with your Holy Spirit and keep me from evil spirits that plague the flesh." It is a way in which we learn to identify who we are in Christ and shed the flesh and the sinful weight it brings.

Sometimes I just repeat the name of Jesus over and over; The Bible says the devils flee just at the sound of His Holy name. I focus on all He is and ask Him to flood my every cell with His presence. The Bible tells us that when we seek the kingdom of heaven first, all other things will fall into place. This brings us up from the world around us and into the realm of glory. The world will cause burdens to hold us down. The Lord will raise us up above the grip of the evil one and protect us when we ask. He loves to show us His power and love. We praise Him in being willing participants as vessels of His will. It is so simple to do. Just stop and talk to Him. He already knows what you need. But when you speak it out, it helps you understand where you are putting your trust and priority, and God will never fail you.

In conclusion, this is not an autobiography of my life. There is plenty of sin and regret between the lines of this life. My niece gave me my mom's little rocker, and here it sits, reminding me what a sinner I am. However, the story contains the important parts through which I learned that there is one God, He gave His Son to die in my place, and He *loves* me beyond human understanding. It is not where you practice your faith or the building you walk in to hold worship to do so but the belief you *hold in your heart.* Make no mistake: there is only *one true God* –the Triune God, the God who loves us unconditionally. I challenge you to ask Him to reveal Himself to you.

Some of the parts of my life that were most defined through His grace are in these pages. The story never ends. My life continues with much heartache over the world and how it impacts my family. But now I know without a doubt that Jesus loves my family members far more than I could ever do, and *He* will not let them go. He will bring them unto Him, and they will share the joy of knowing Him as their Savior. The love we must give to save others sometimes causes disruption in the earthly realms, but when we pray and God works through us, we know that whatever happens, God is in control and that He will deliver us.

Prayer is so vital, so necessary to keep above the fray of what the world is delivering. Satan is a liar and a deceiver. Do not let him

A DIVINE APPOINTMENT

have any attention. He will do his best to make us think our feelings and problems come first. No, Jesus does, and Jesus will gladly take the problems. Remember a few pages ago I mentioned that I told God I would gladly take the pain it did any good for anyone? Well, I learned I don't have to take it; Jesus already has, for *all* of us. God has been telling me to prepare. He said He is coming back soon. I believe something is about to happen. I look forward to seeing you in heaven, Just tell Jesus you know you are a sinner and that you want Him to come into your heart and be your Lord. You are ready to do His will, and He will welcome you into the family of saints. God is waiting.

You have *A Divine Appointment!*